CAT COLORING BOOK

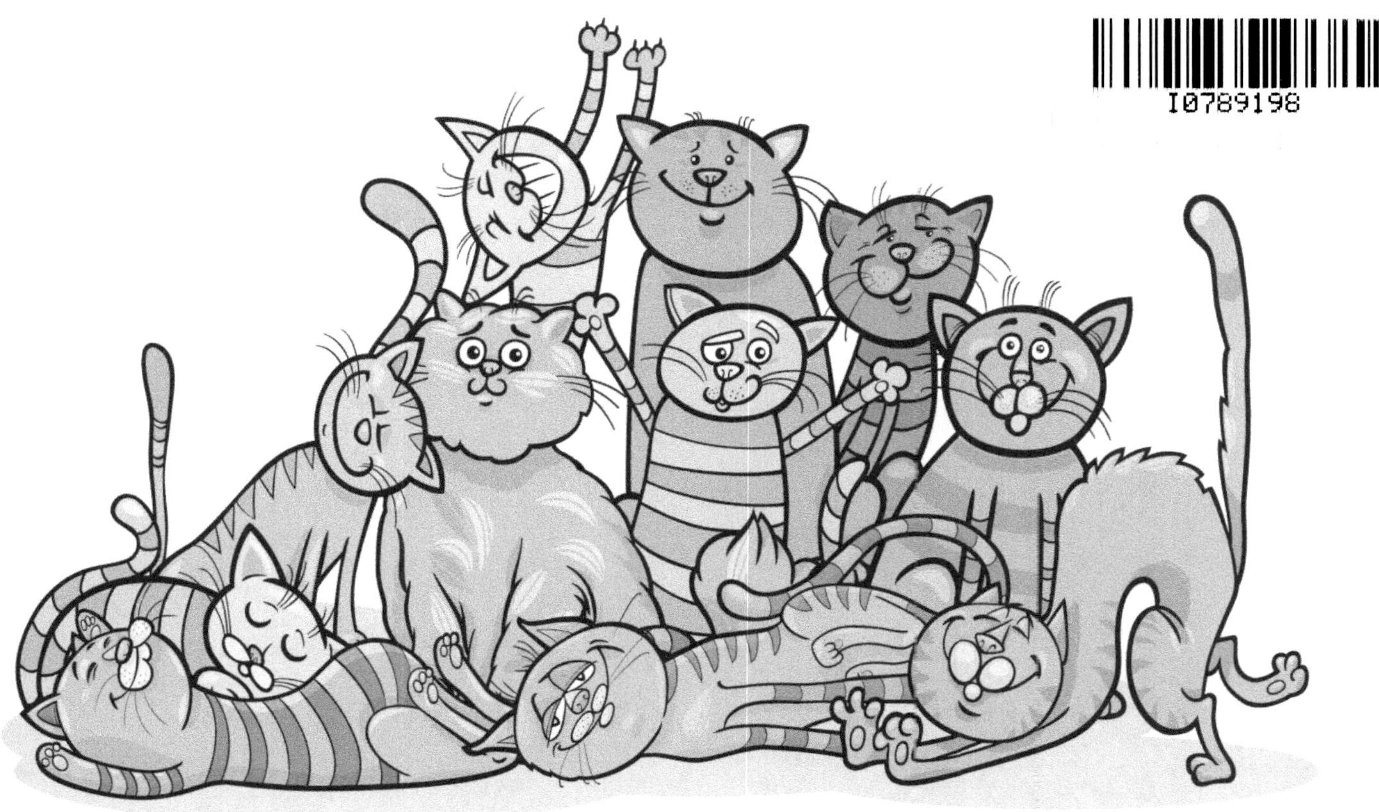

THIS BOOK BELONG TO ....

....

....

....

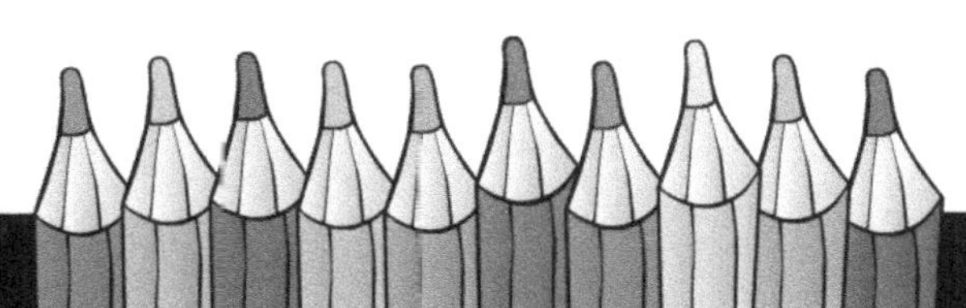

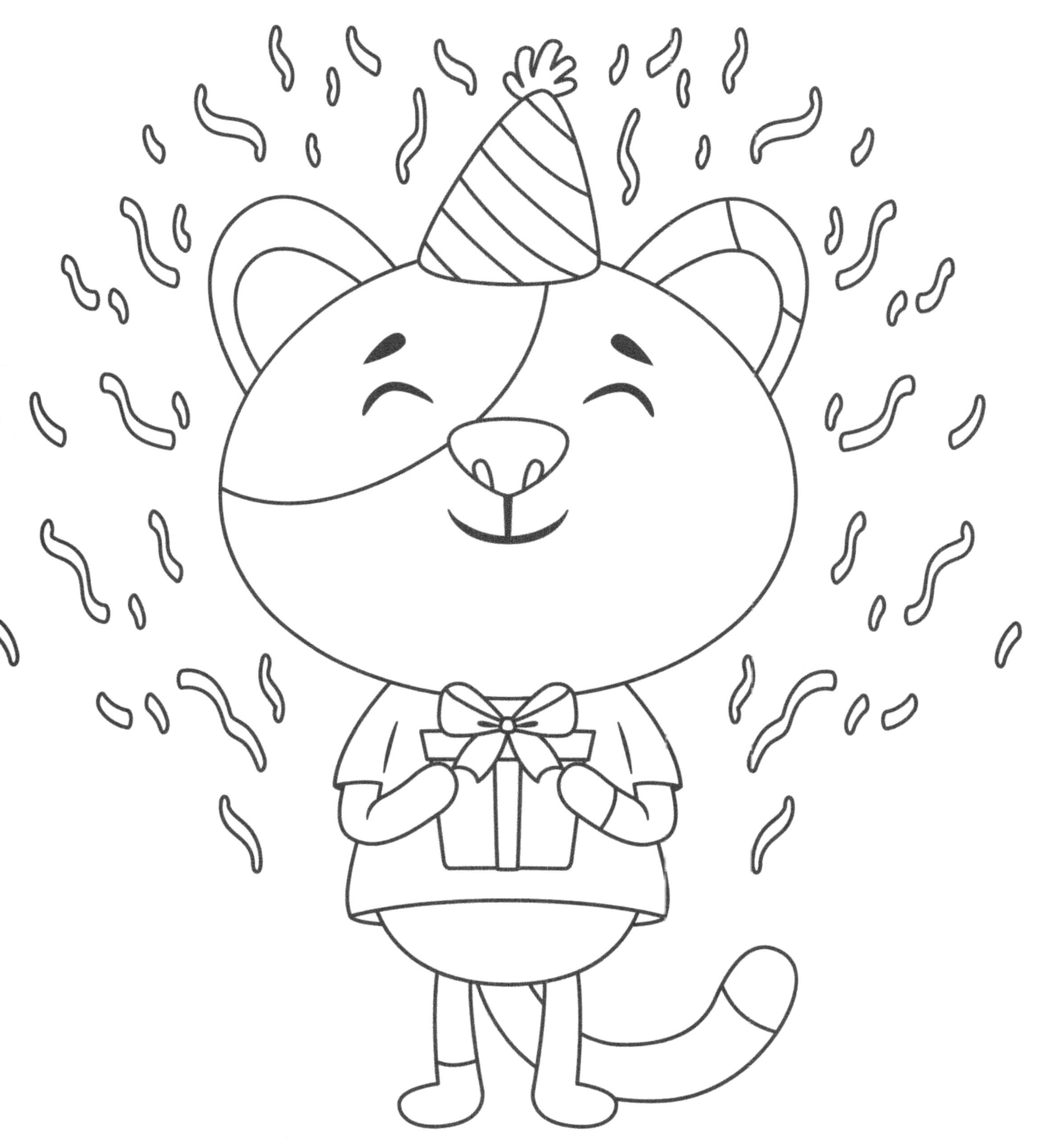

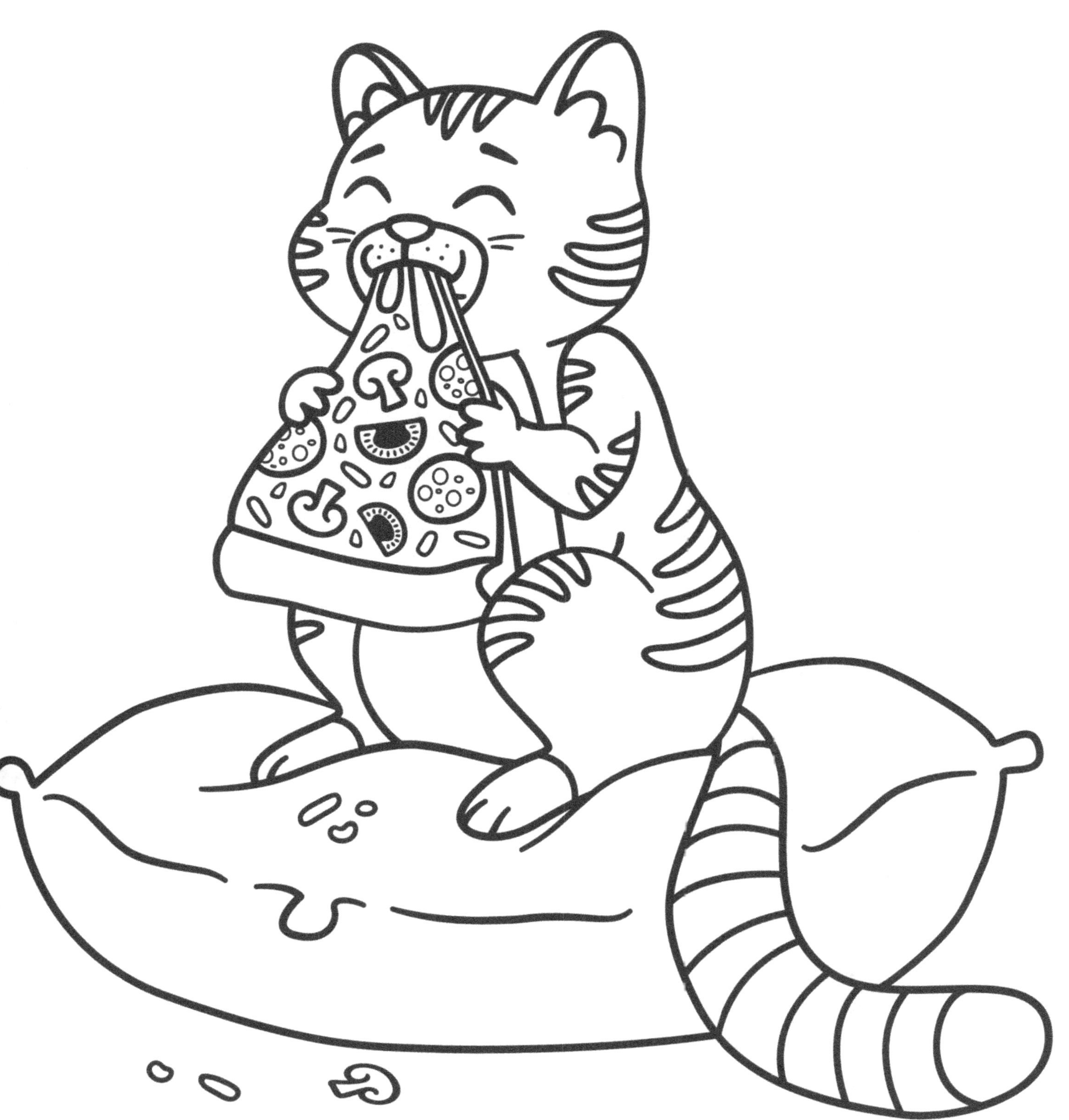

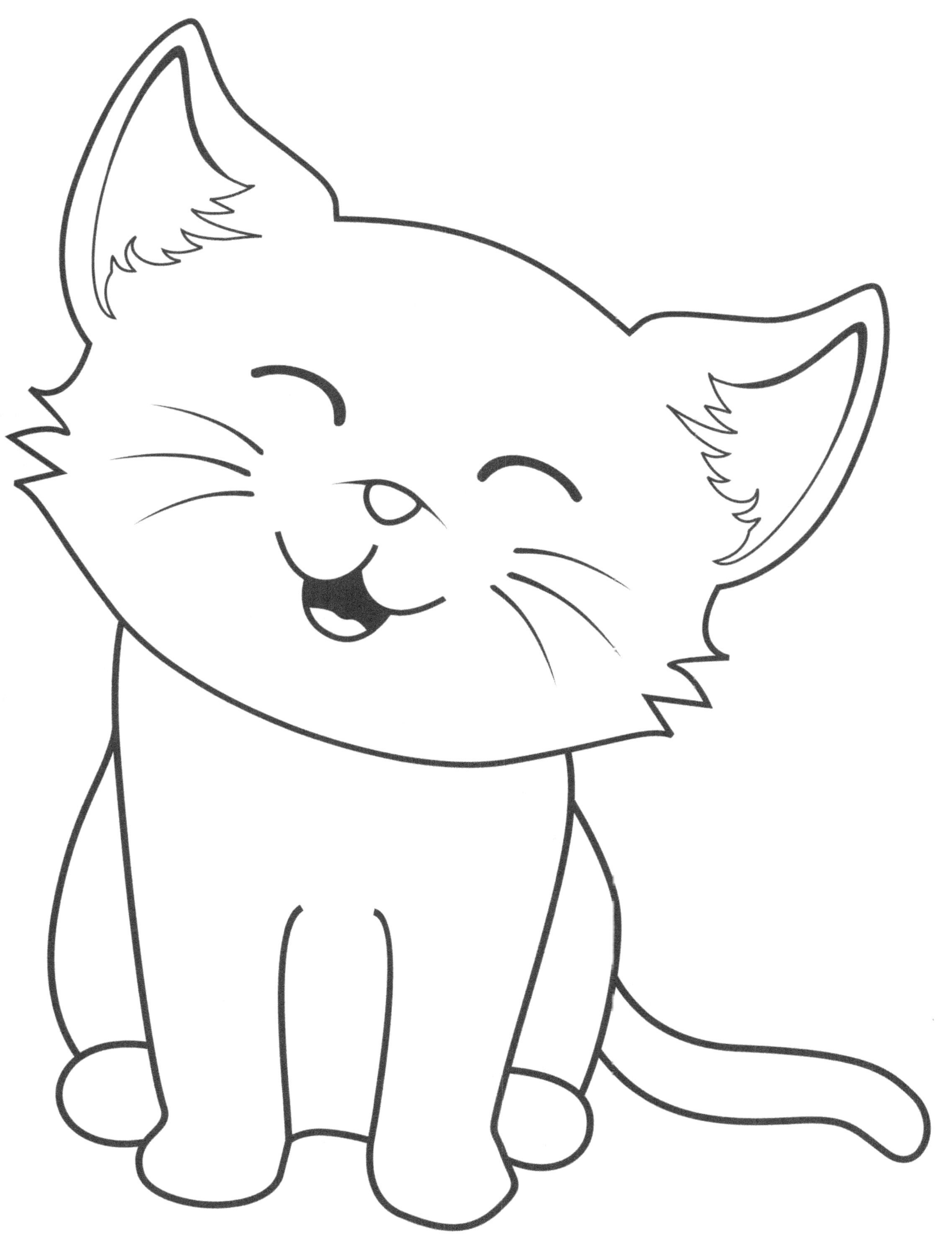

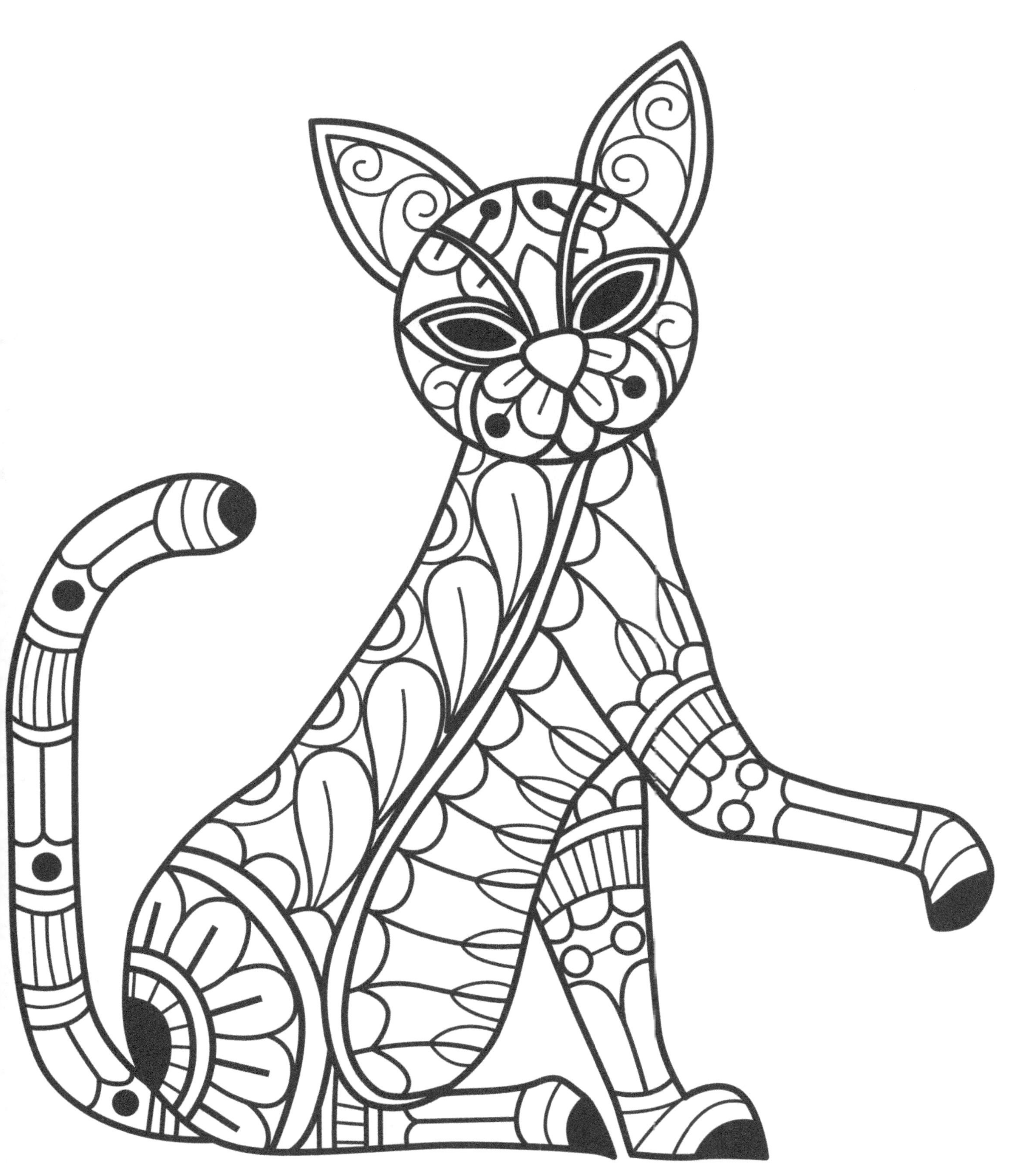

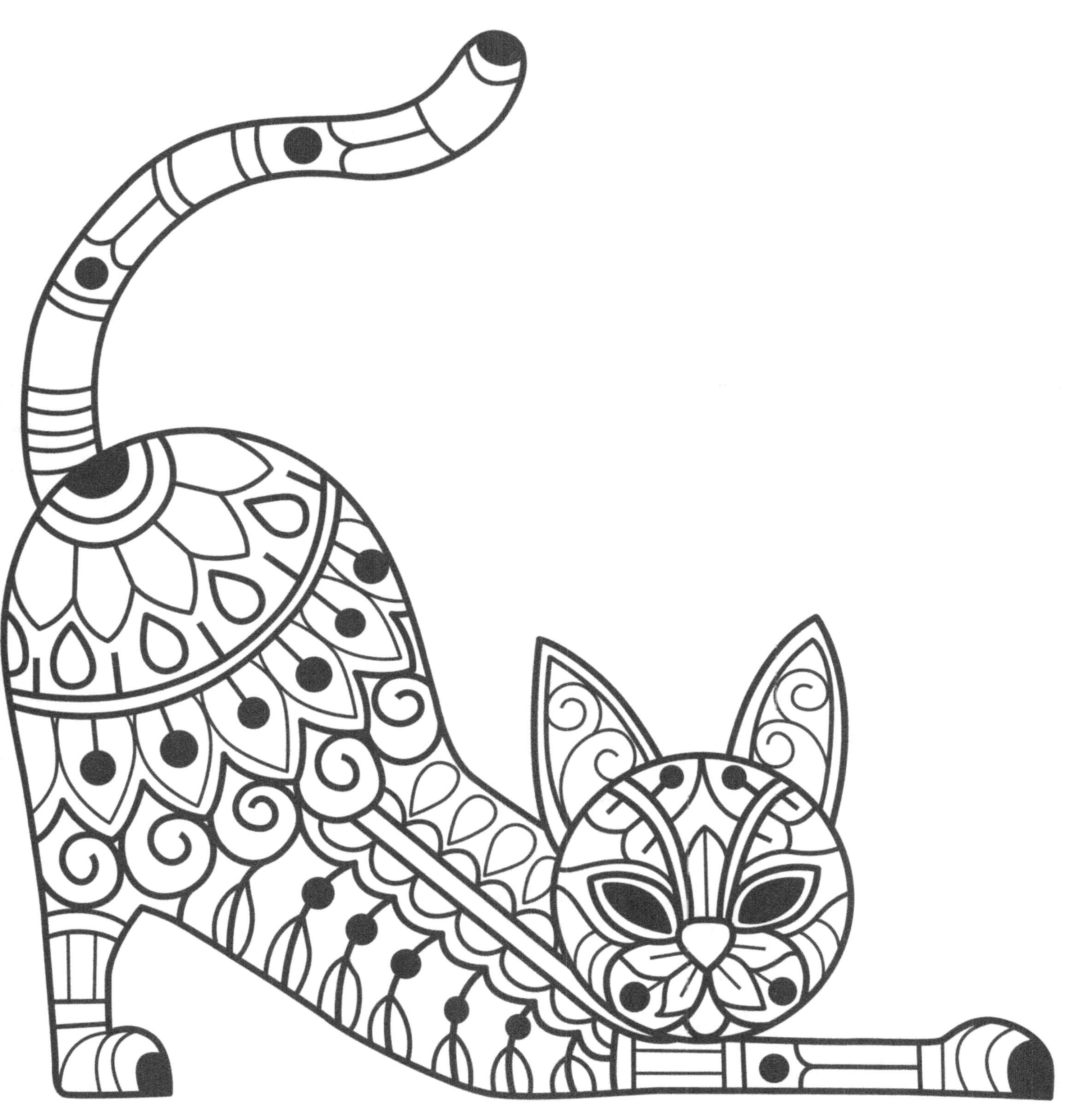

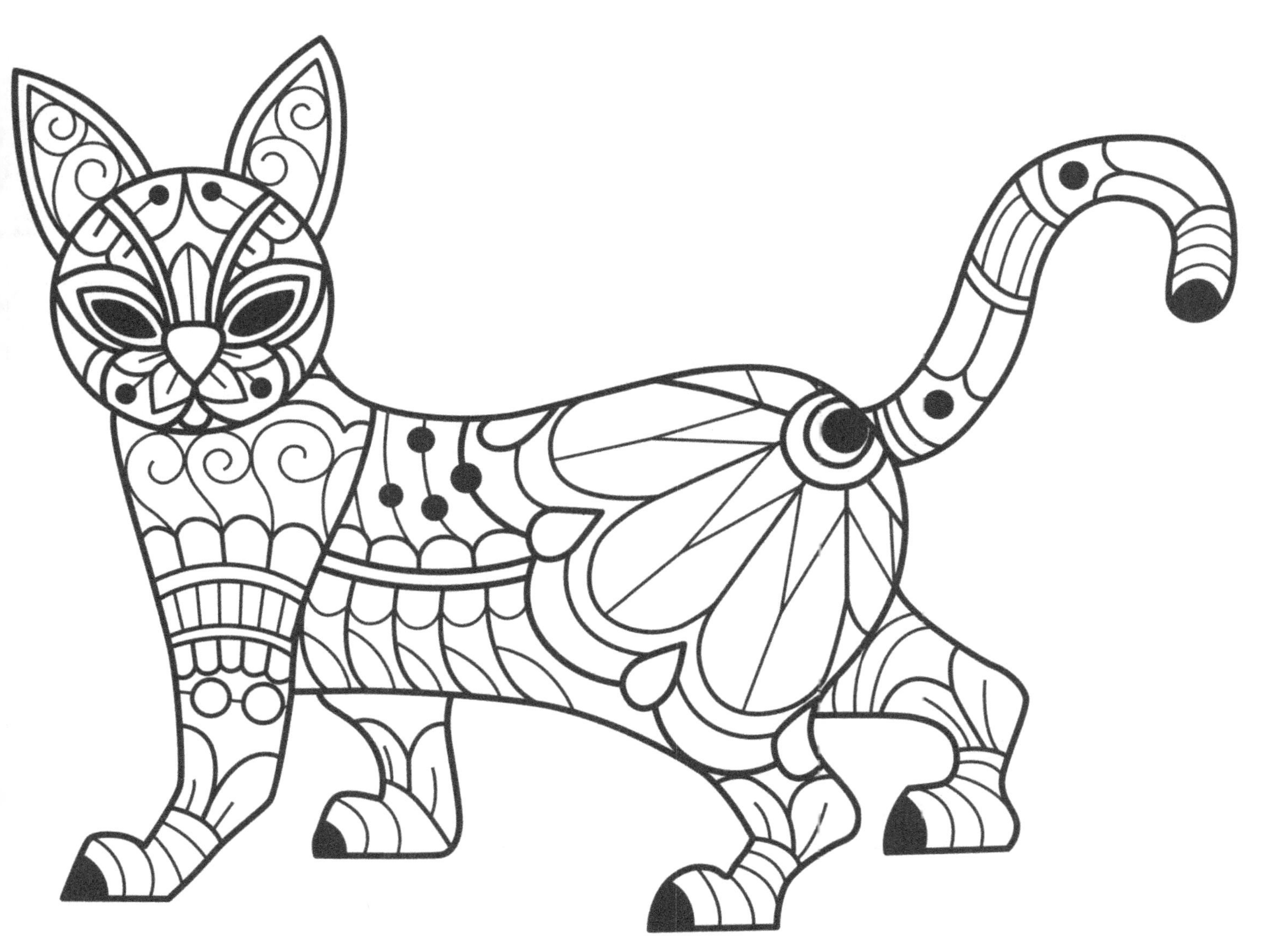

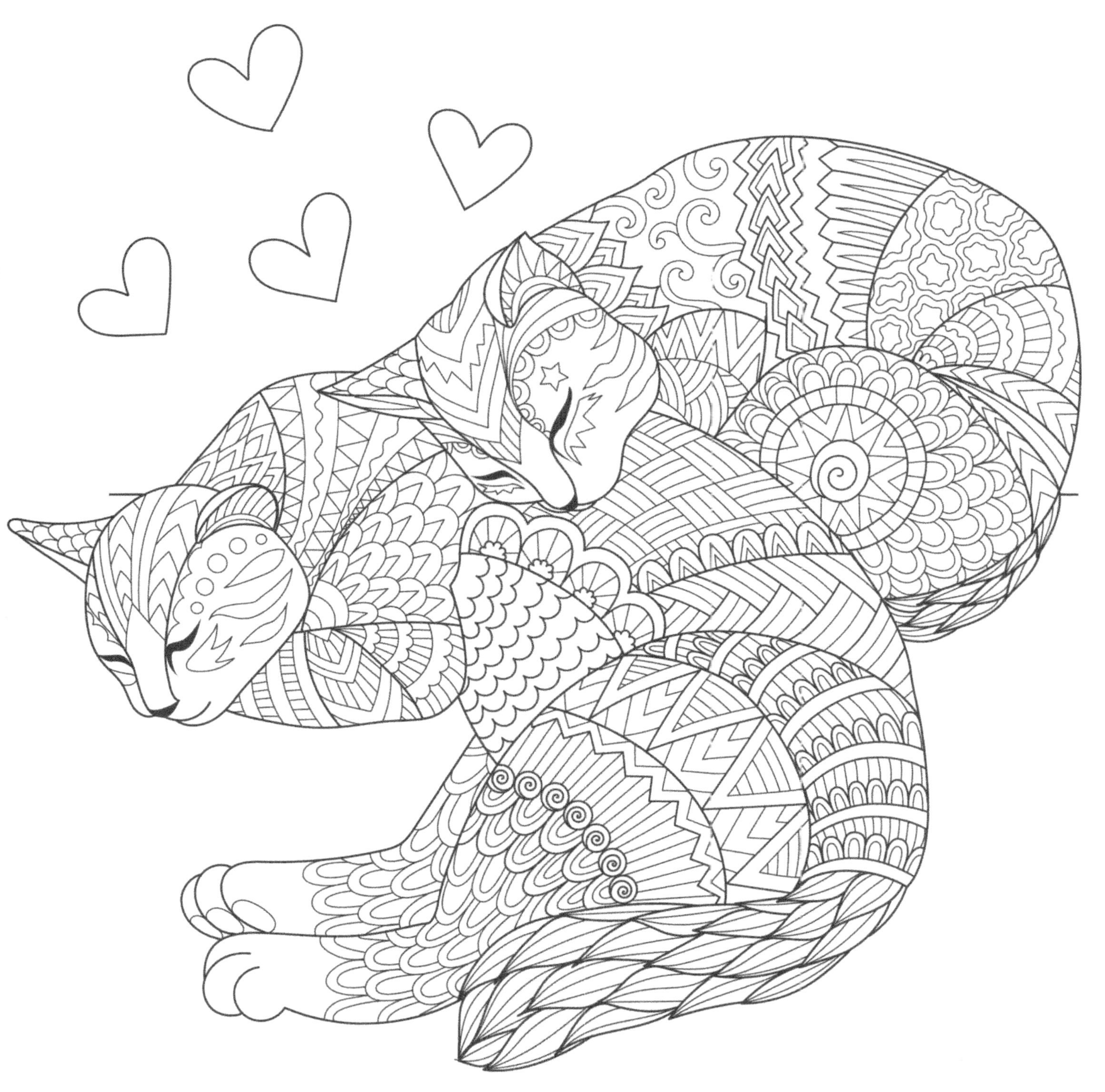

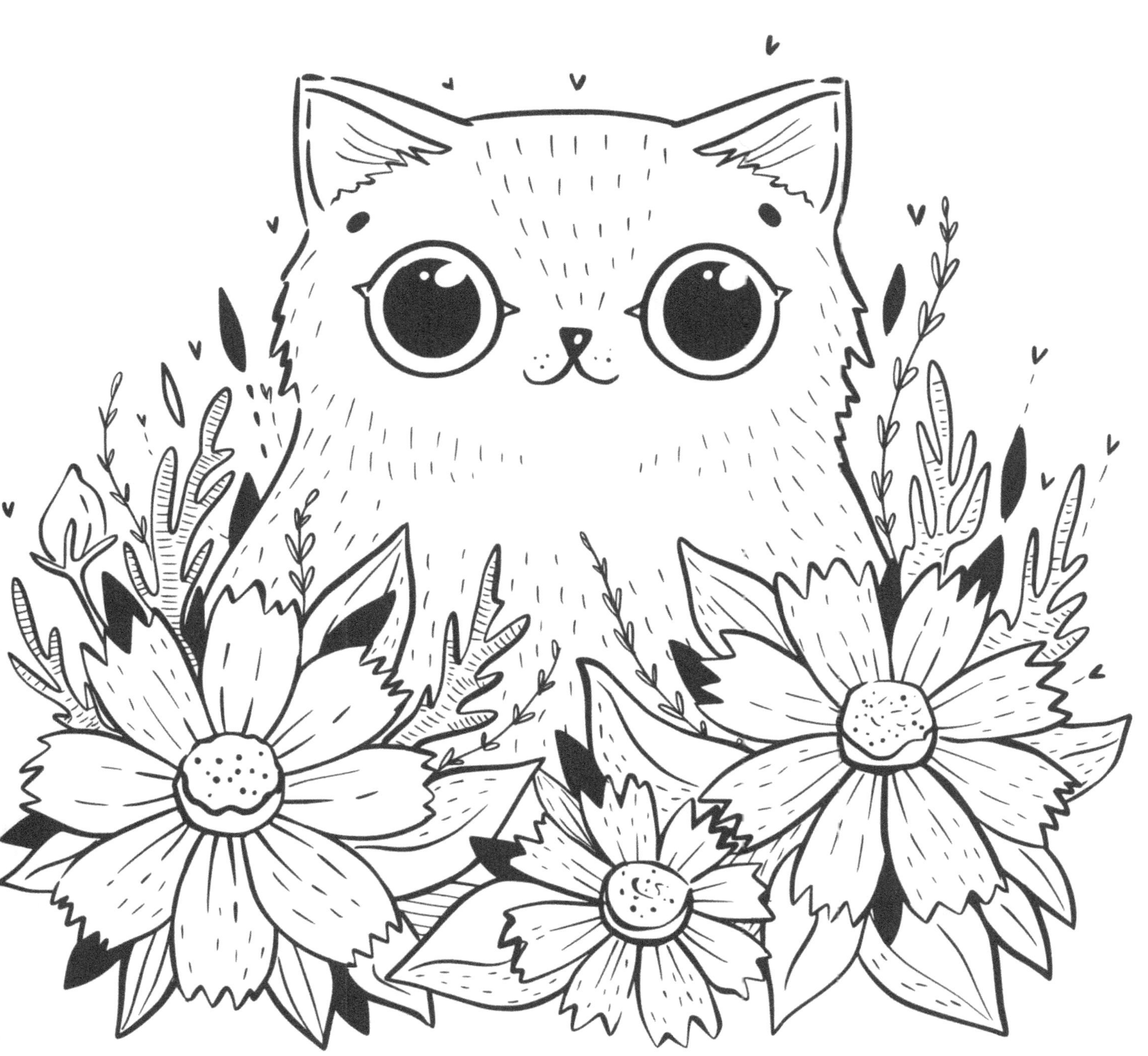

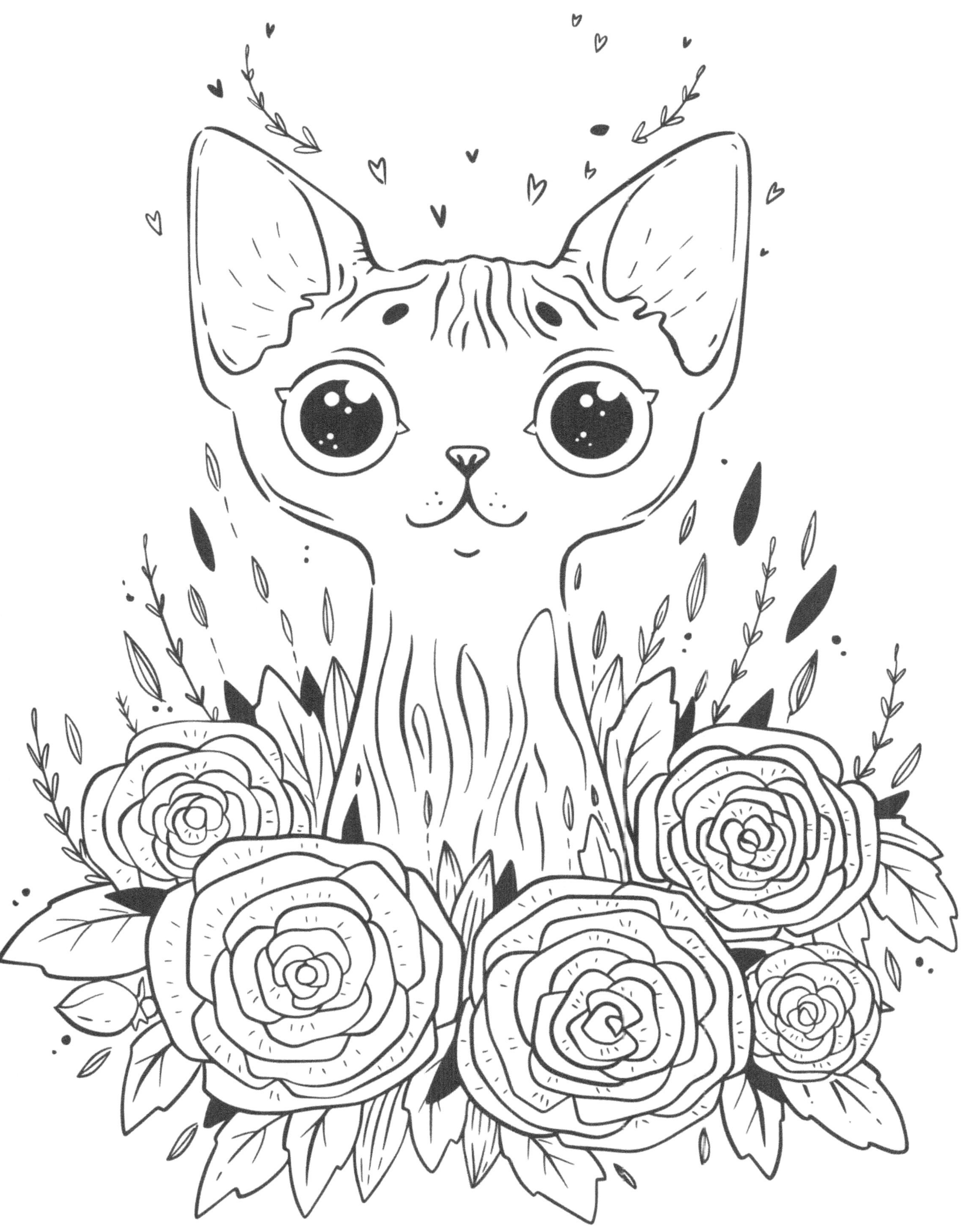

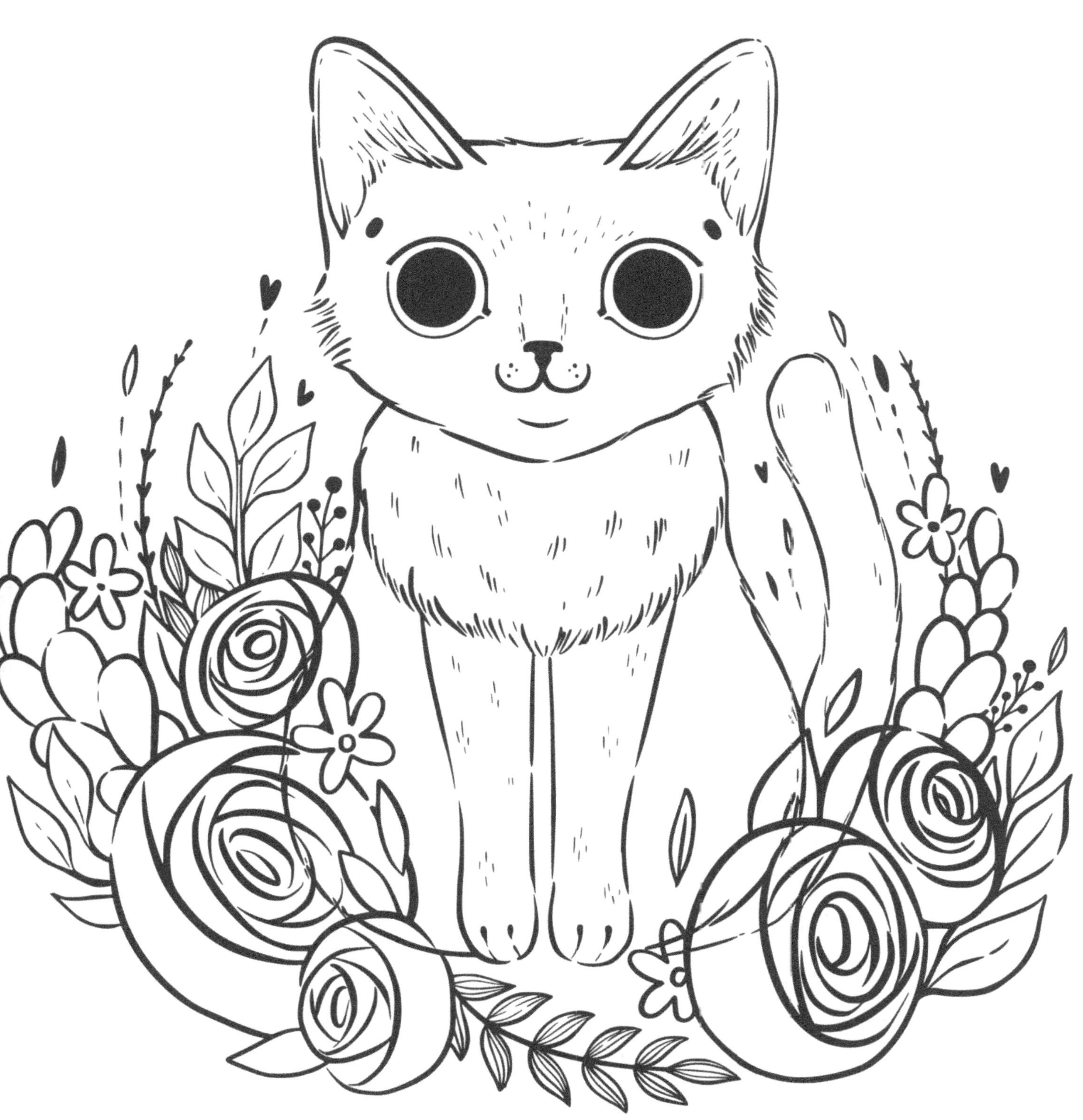

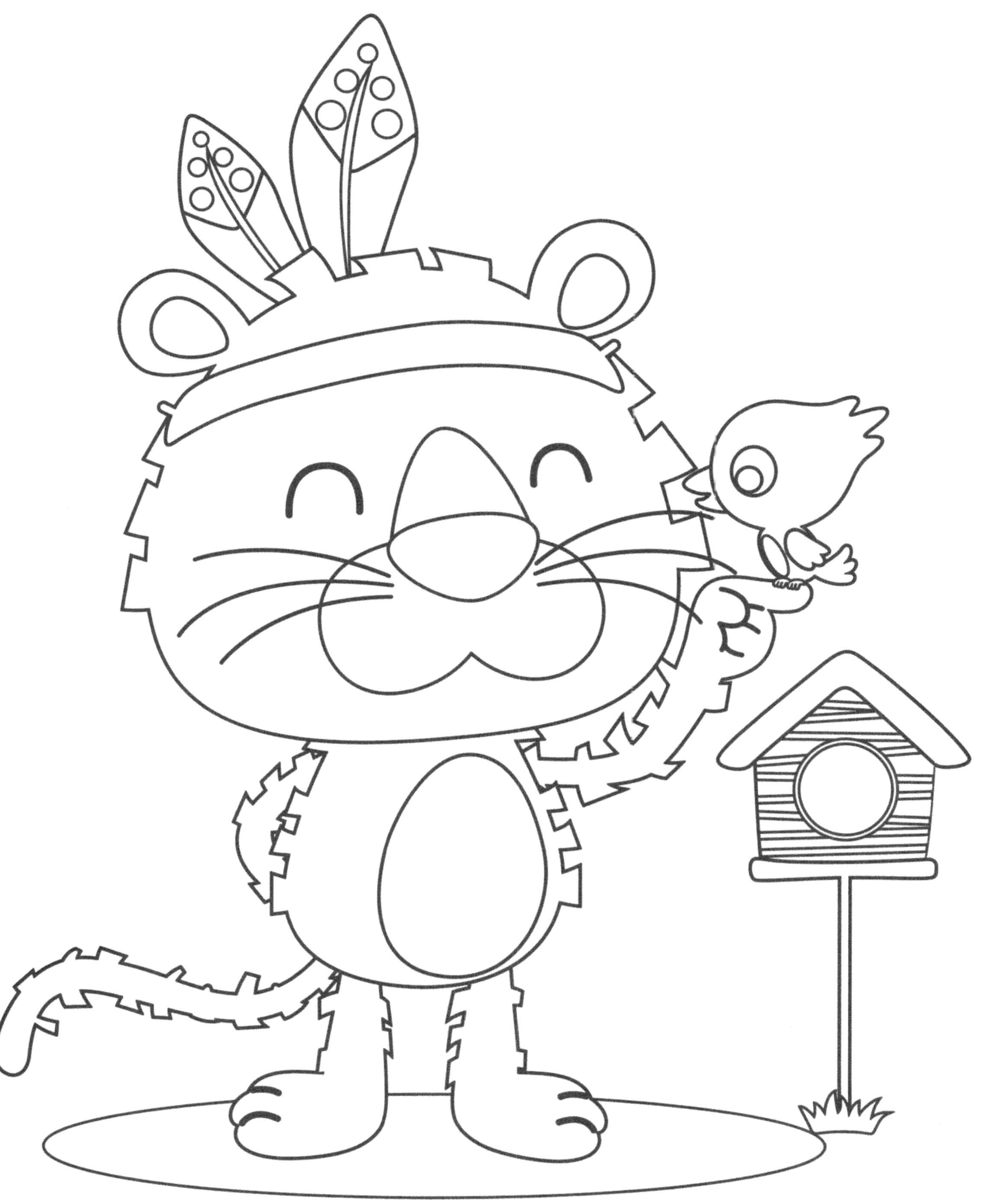

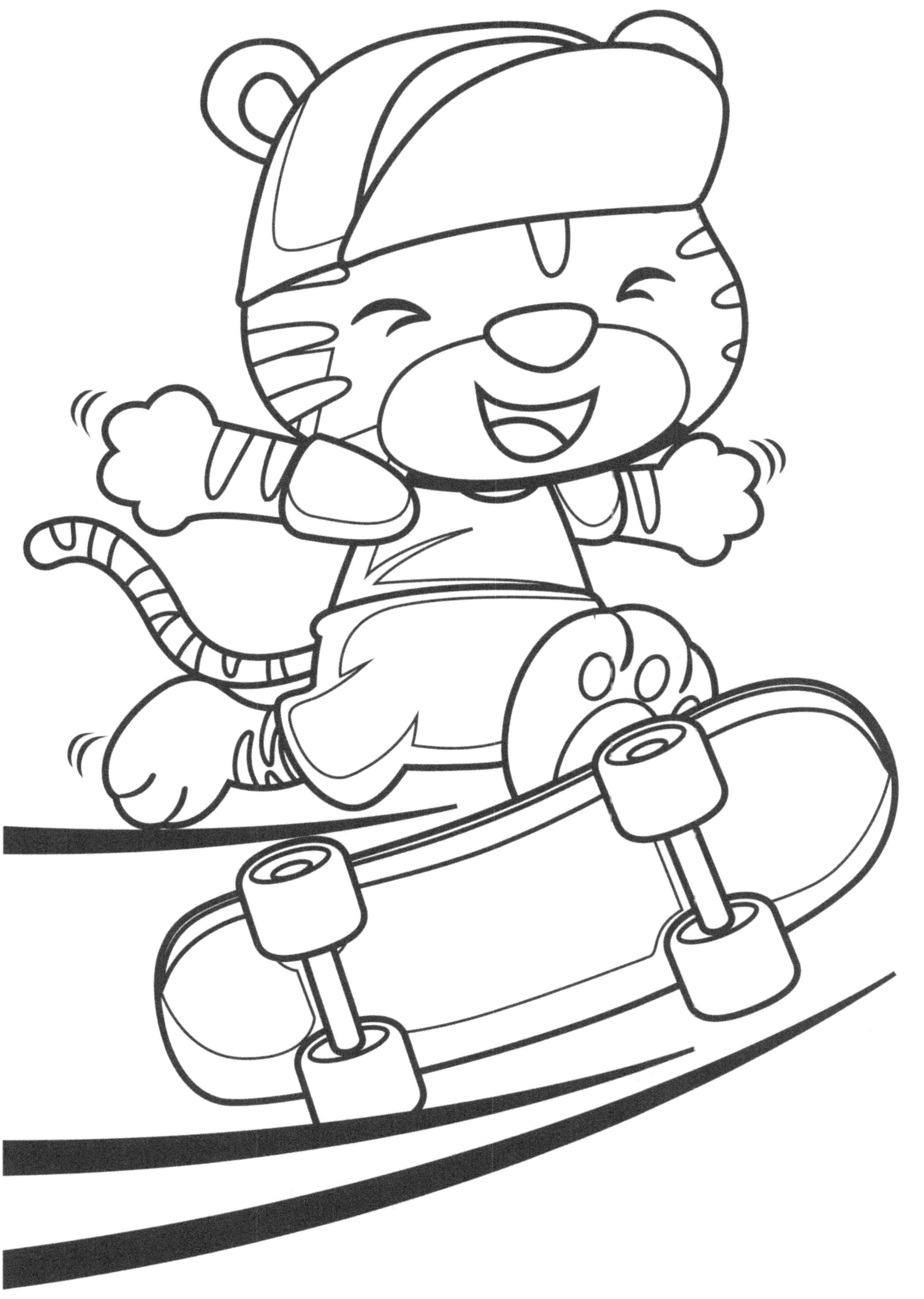

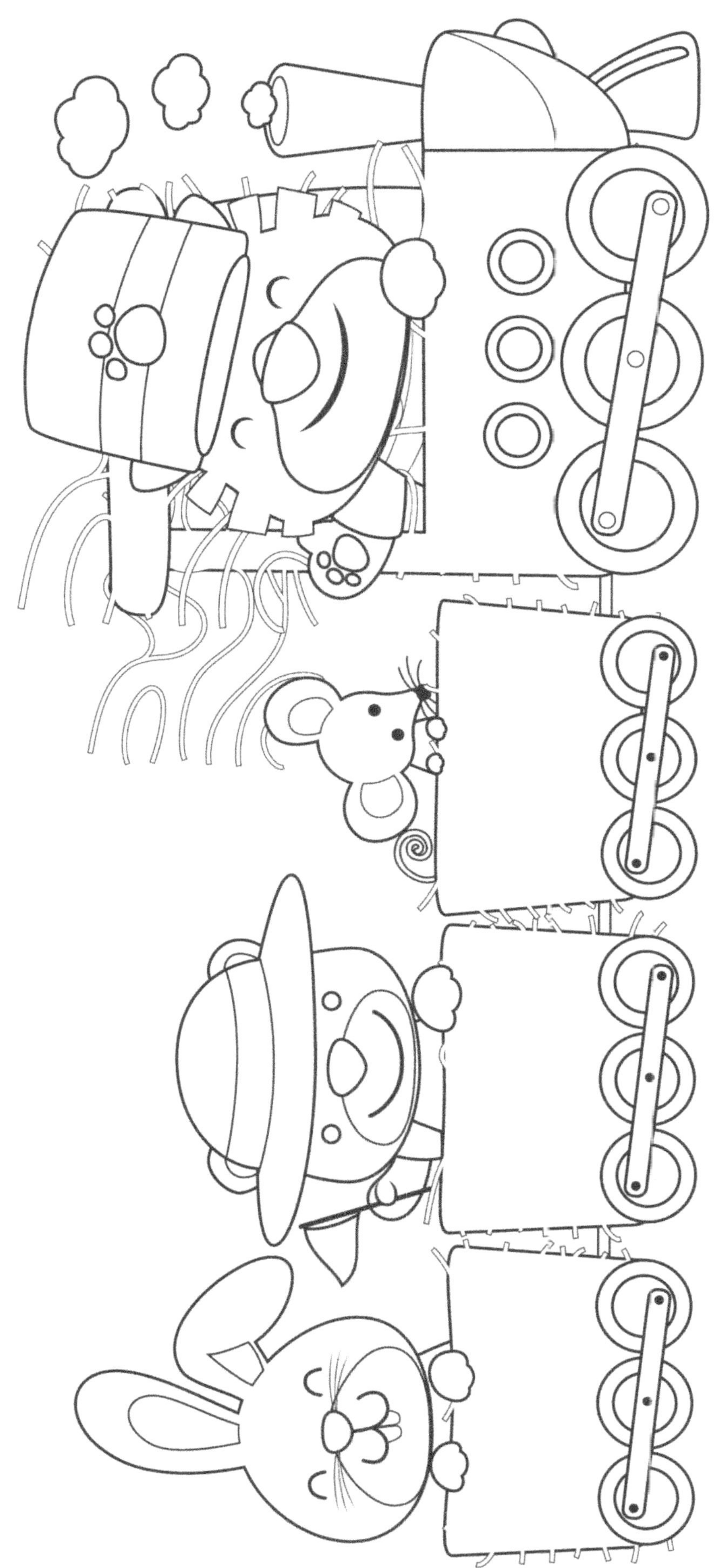

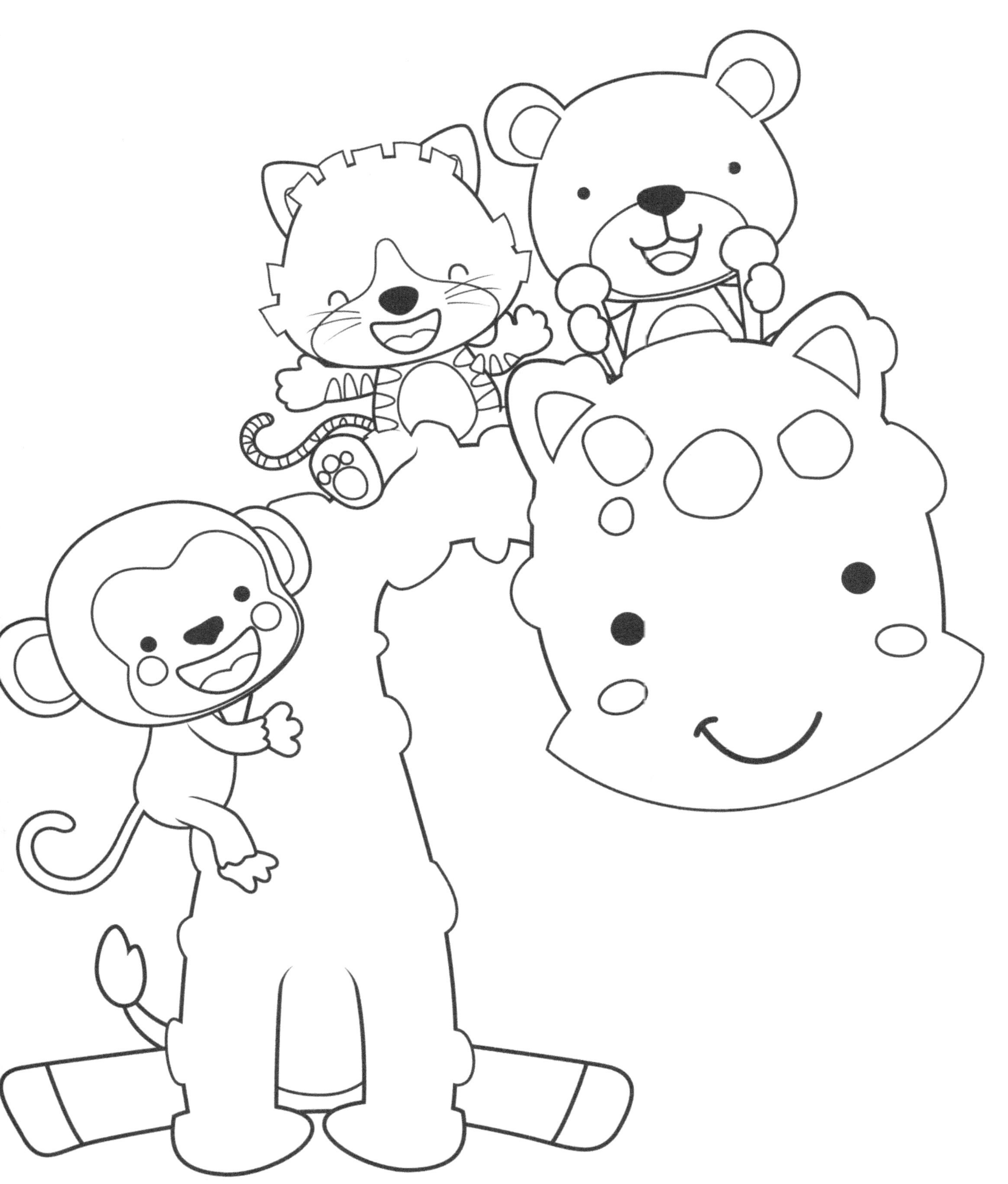

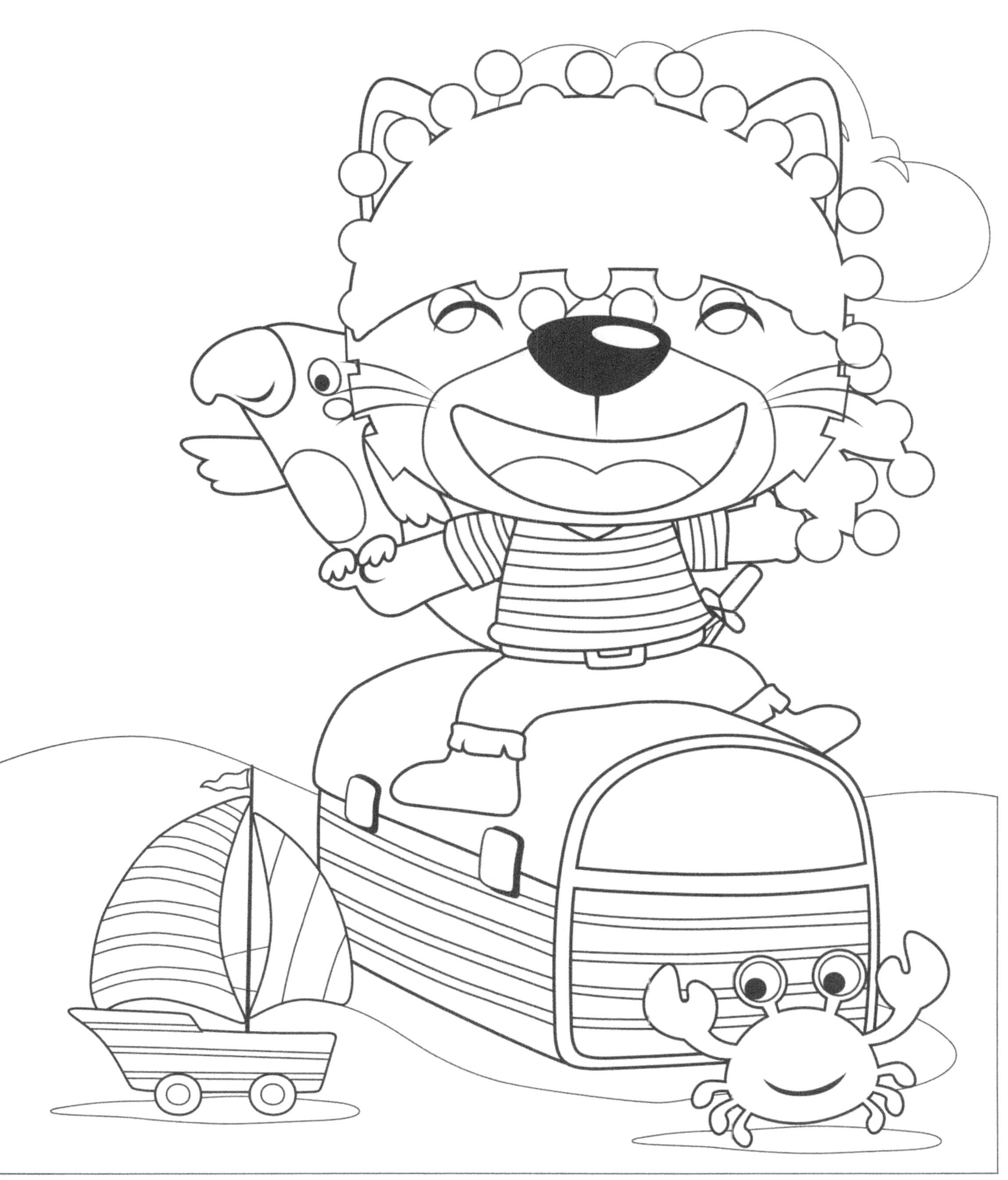

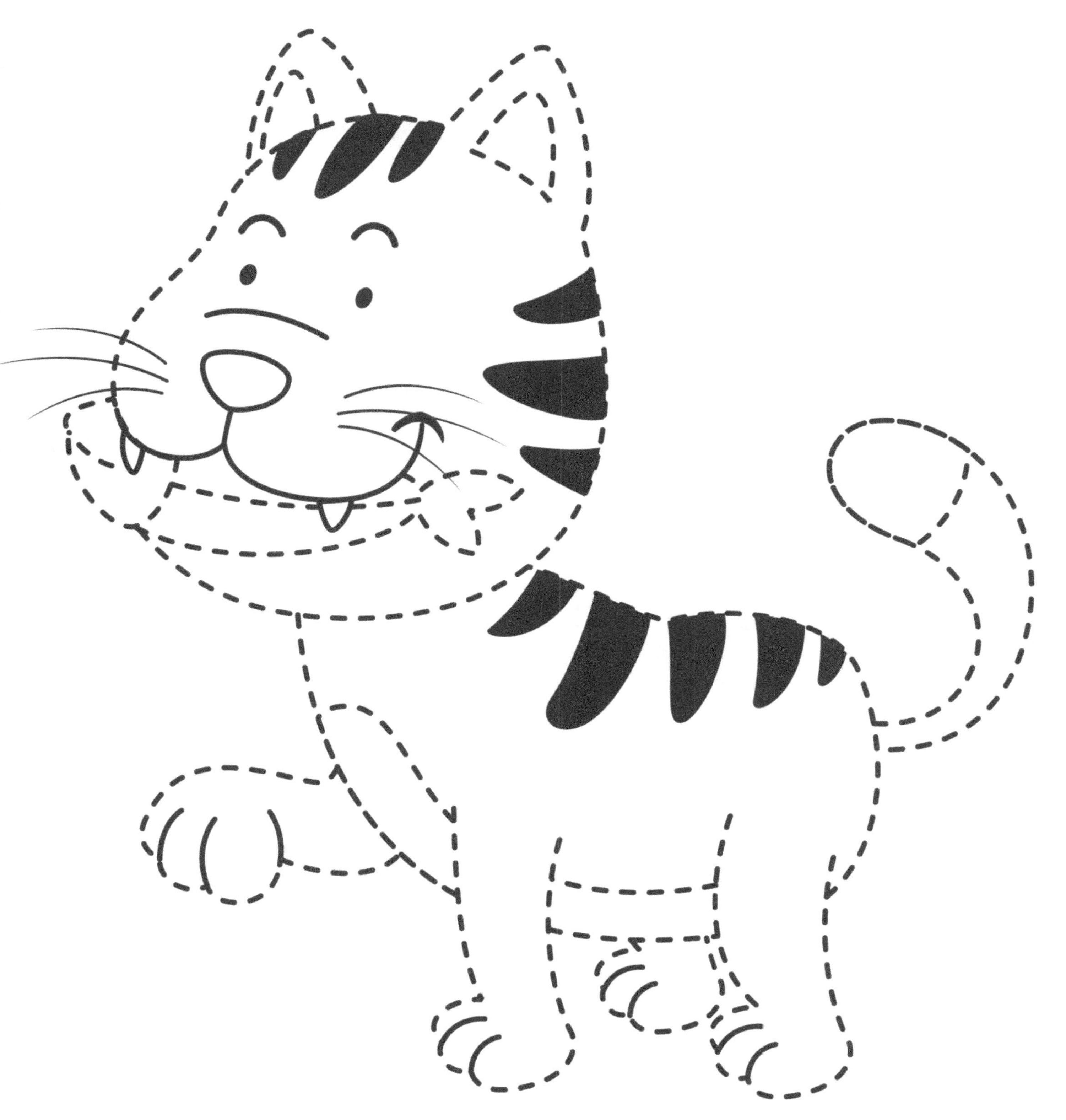

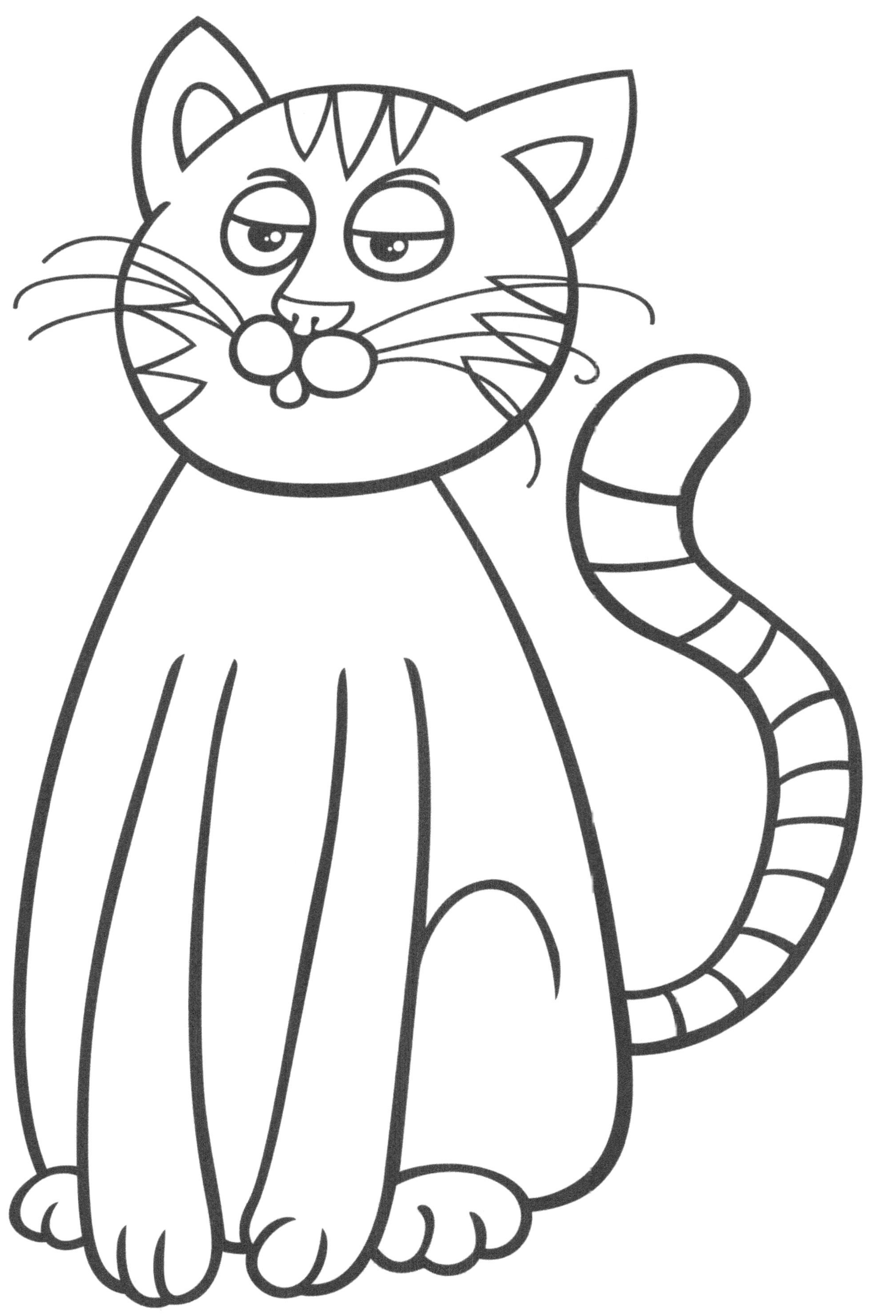

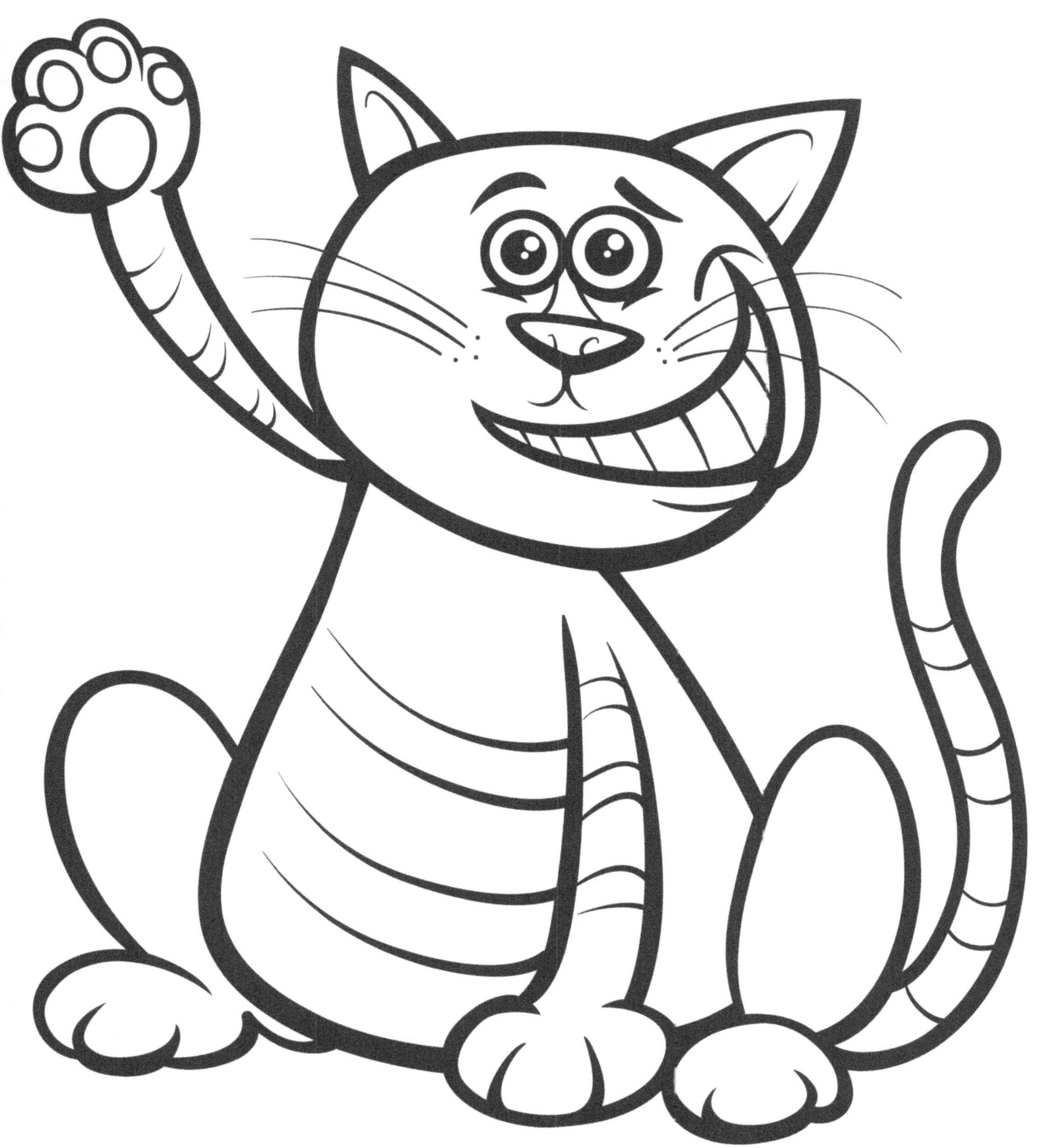

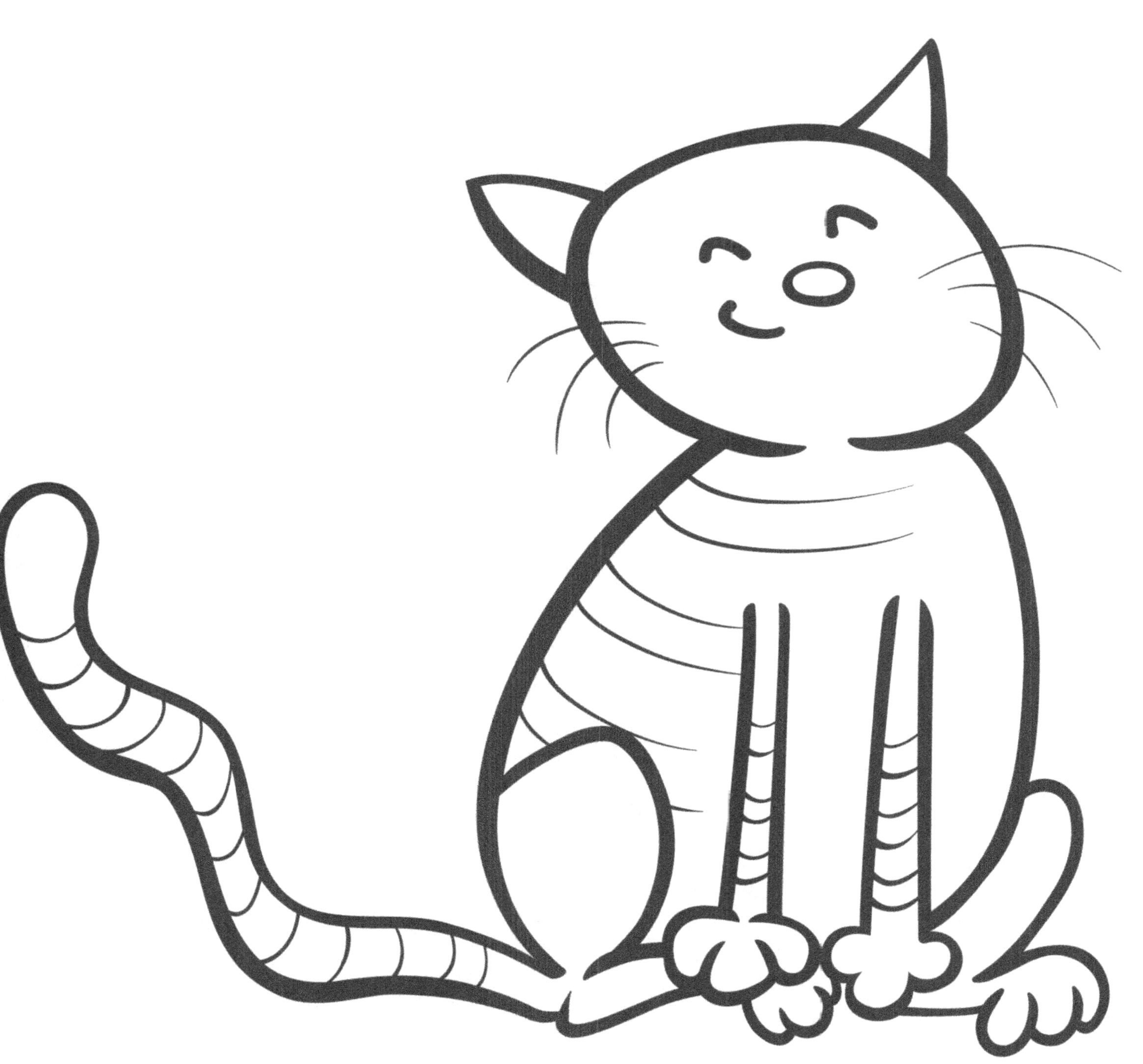

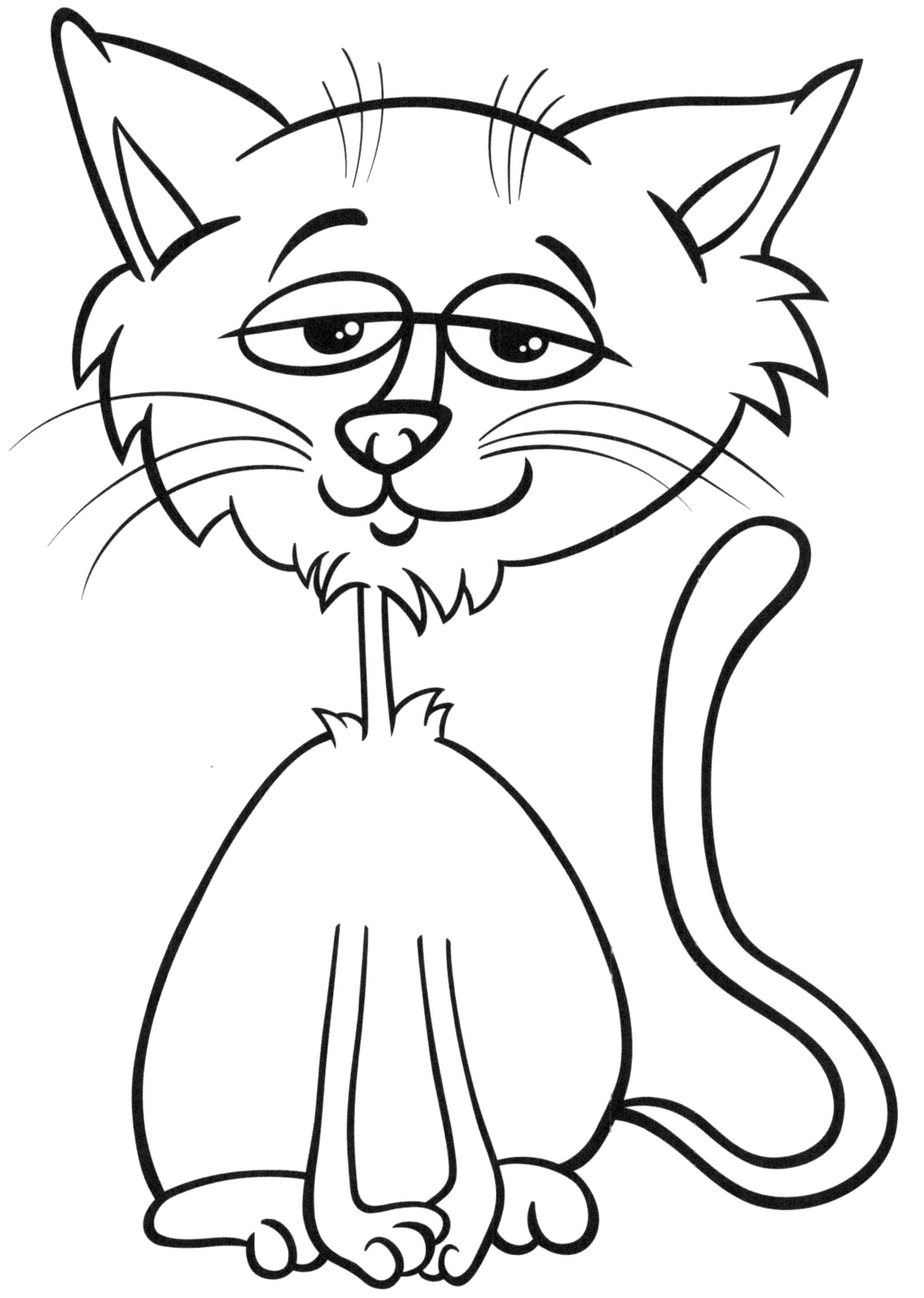

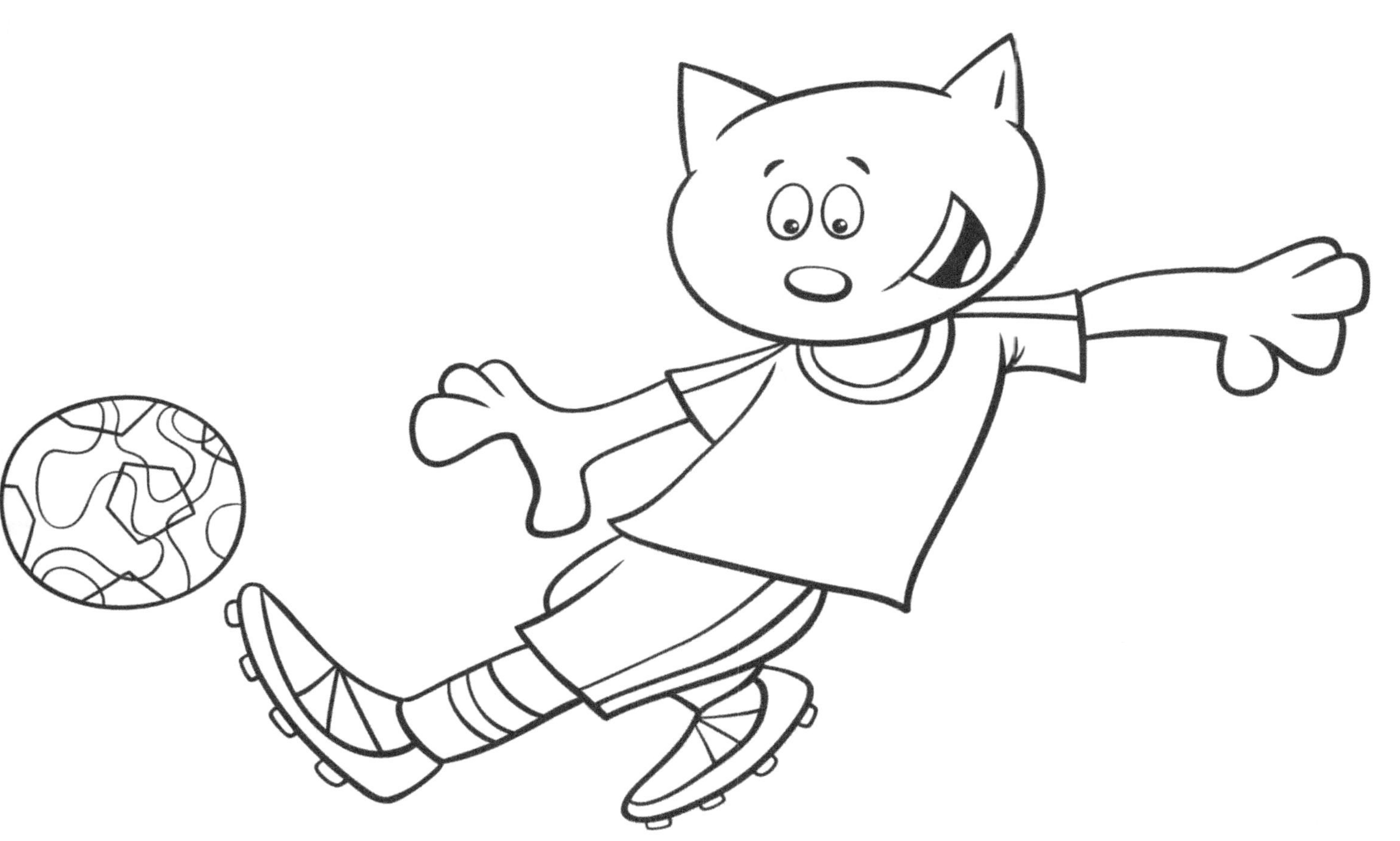

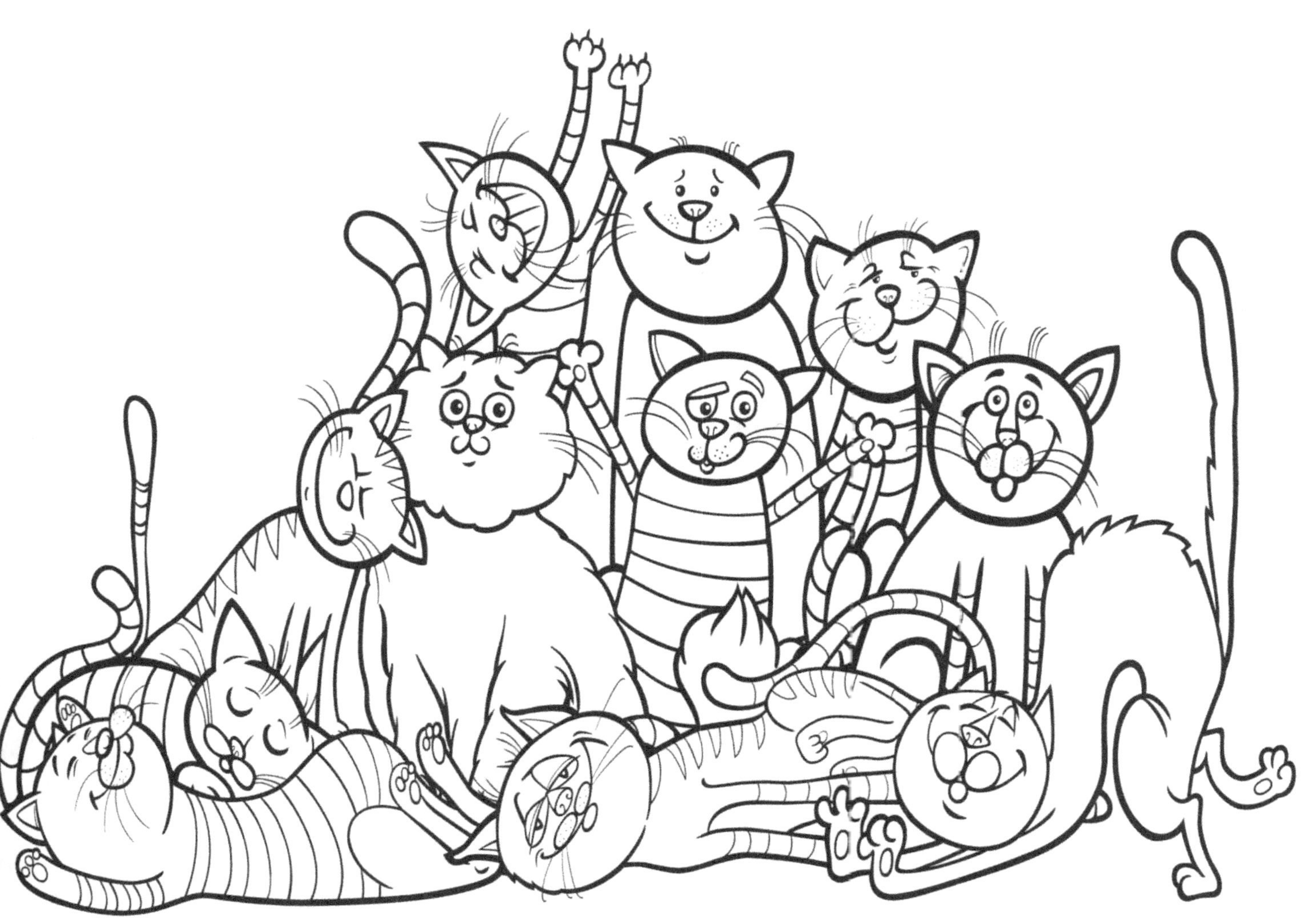

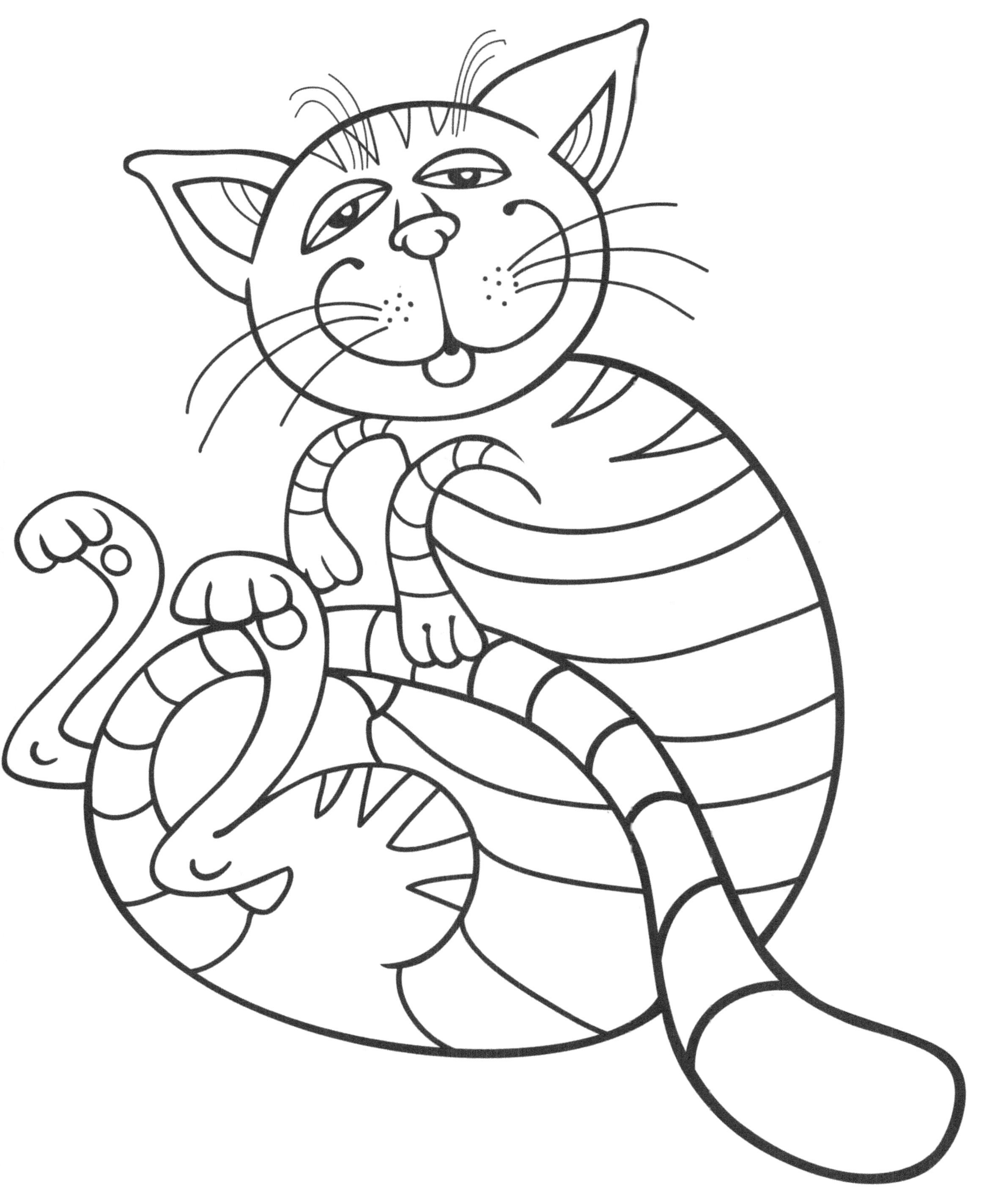

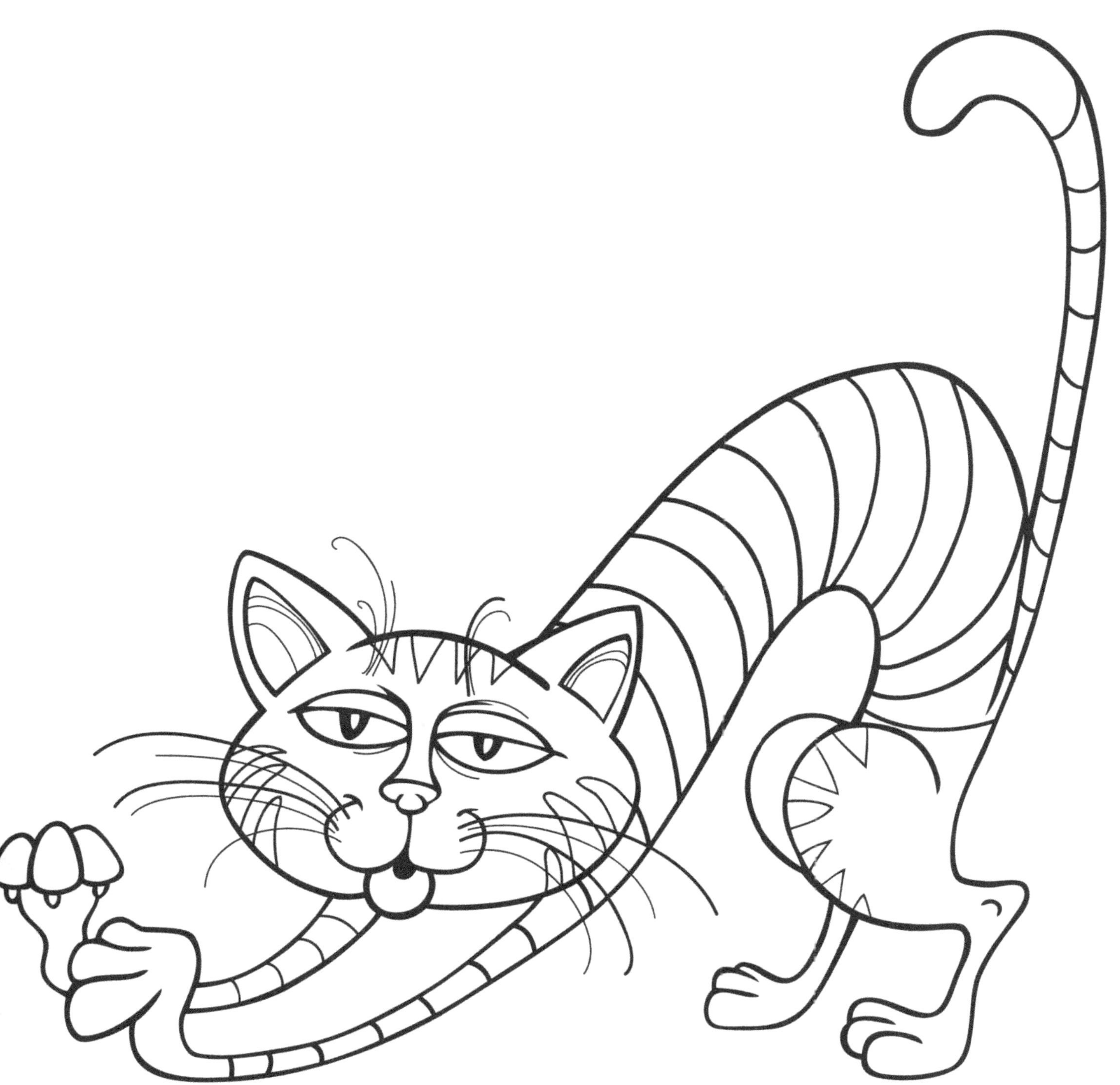